The Industrial Revolution in England

By
R. M. HARTWELL
Fellow of Nuffield College, Oxford

The publication of a pamphlet by the Historical Association does not necessarily imply the Association's official approbation of the opinions expressed therein

THE INDUSTRIAL REVOLUTION IN ENGLAND

I

REVOLUTIONS of the magnitude of the industrial revolution in England provoke historical controversy: such a revolution is a major discontinuity which a profession more skilled in explaining small changes finds difficult to understand. A revolution that touches a whole society is so diffuse that its significant events are difficult to identify: the causes, course and consequences, immediate and long-term, are so complex, and involve so many people in such different ways, that it tends to be interpreted, not in the light of objective analysis, but as the support of some interest or ideology. The industrial revolution in England is no exception. There is a widely held assumption that what was distinctive and what was changing in England between 1750 and 1850 was part of, or the result of, an industrial revolution. J. Steven Watson writes, for example, that by 1815 'it could be claimed that England had been reorientated by economic forces more radically than France by the guillotine and the Code of Napoleon'.[1] And so most history books of this period have their economic chapters, accounts of the changing technology and organization of agriculture and industry, of the growth of population, of the triumph of *laissez faire* and the middle classes, of the social consequences of industrial change. However, the link with general history is usually tenuously drawn, and more interesting than the familiar catalogues of industrial information are the gaps in knowledge and the conflicts in opinion that all accounts of the industrial revolution, especially by economic historians, display.

On the causes of the industrial revolution, for example, there is silence, simplicity or confusion. What was the prime mover, or what complex of movers was responsible? Agricultural revolution? Population growth? Improved technology? Increasing trade? Capital accumulation? All these have their supporters. Or must the explanation be sought in non-economic forces? Changes in religion, social structure, science, philosophy

1. *The Reign of George III, 1760–1815*, The Oxford History of England, Vol. 12, Oxford University Press, 1960, p. 503.

continuity + change

and law? It is impossible not to agree with Professor A. Redford, writing in 1960: 'The causes of the movement known as "the industrial revolution" have now been sought by scholars for nearly three generations, and as yet there seems to be little agreement as to why the rapid increase in the rate of economic development which marked the period 1760–1830 in England should occur when it did.'[1] More surprising, perhaps, is our ignorance of the men who pioneered and carried through the industrial revolution. Except for the great captains, about whom there is sufficient information to make generalization difficult, little is known of the entrepreneurs. What sort of men were they? What were their social origins? Where did they get capital? What did they develop into? 'The evidence remains too flimsy and incomplete', Professor Charles Wilson has written of the industrial revolution entrepreneurs, 'to conclude with confidence more than this: that they came from every social source and every area.'[2] There is not even agreement about the time period subsumed under the term 'industrial revolution'. When did the revolution begin? In 1740, 1760 or 1780? When did it end? In 1830, 1850 or even later? What were the important turning points between whatever are the appropriate terminal dates? 1760 to 1830 has been the most acceptable revolutionary period, but Phyllis Deane and W. A. Cole have suggested recently that there was 'a marked acceleration in the rate of growth after 1745',[3] and J. H. Clapham reminded us long ago that not a single English industry had been through a complete revolution in technology by 1850.[4]

The largest literature of disagreement, however, is on the losses or gains of industrialization. Was the economic gain greater than the social loss? What happened to the standard of living of the urban and agricultural workers during the industrial revolution? Was it rising with national wealth, or was

1. *The Economic History of England, 1760–1860*, London, 2nd ed., 1960, p. 3.

2. 'The Entrepreneur in the Industrial Revolution in Britain', *History*, Vol. XLII (1957), p. 112.

3. *British Economic Growth, 1688–1959. Trends and Structure*, Cambridge University Press, 1962, p. 79.

4. *An Economic History of Modern Britain. Free Trade and Steel, 1850–1886*, Cambridge University Press, 1932, Ch. III.

it falling with increasing inequality and exploitation?[1] Finally there is the problem, as yet unanswered, indeed hardly explored, of the influence of the industrial revolution on art and literature. The relationship with politics is assumed but rarely analysed, and, as R. H. Tawney has pointed out, 'We know at present next to nothing of the relations between the artistic achievements of an epoch and the character of its economic life, and the only candid course is to confess that if, as seems probable, such elusive links exist, the secret of their interaction is as yet beyond our grasp.'[2]

In this pamphlet we mean by 'the industrial revolution of England' the changes in English industry, and their impact on the English economy and society, between the beginning of the sharp upward movement in industrial production in 1780 and the end of the first period of great structural change of the economy in 1850. Thus defined the industrial revolution becomes an example of economic growth, the first of those remarkable changes in economy that over the last two centuries have turned a large proportion of the world's population from farmers into producers of manufactured goods and services.

II

The idea of 'the industrial revolution' owes its modern popularity to Arnold Toynbee's *Lectures on the Industrial Revolution of the Eighteenth Century in England*, published in 1884. As a term it was used as early as 1837 by Blanqui. As an idea to describe and explain the economic transformation of England there was realization even before this of the strategic importance of the revolutionary changes that had been occurring in industry since some time in the eighteenth century. Indeed, the first writers who saw the industrial revolution as a phenomenon that needed explanation sought its origins in the revolution in industrial technology, in the actions of the inventors of the new machines; they saw as the essence of the industrial revolution the harnessing of new machines to new sources of power in new industrial units, the factories. 'Our engineers', wrote Samuel

1. R. M. Hartwell, 'Interpretations of the Industrial Revolution in England: A Methodological Inquiry', *Journal of Economic History*, Vol. XIX (1959), pp. 229–49.

2. *Social History and Literature*, Leicester University Press, 1958, p. 28.

Smiles, 'may be regarded in some measure as the makers of modern civilization. . . . Are not the men who have made the motive power of the country, and immensely increased its productive strength, the men above all others who have tended to make the country what it is?'[1] A later, more sophisticated version of this theory – a by-product of economic theory and entrepreneurial history – linked invention with innovation and asked why so many important inventions were made in the late eighteenth century, and why and how entrepreneurs were able to exploit these inventions in production; the answers were, on the one hand, the growth of scientific knowledge reaching a critical stage of development, and, on the other, increasingly favourable economic conditions, especially market conditions. After 1850, however, there were also historians who regarded the industrial revolution as the triumph of *laissez faire*. 'The essence of the Industrial Revolution', Toynbee wrote, 'is the substitution of competition for the mediaeval regulations which had previously controlled the production and distribution of wealth.'[2] To Toynbee, as to Thorold Rogers before him, the abandoning of mercantilist restrictions on industry and trade, which had liberated market forces stimulating to industrial enterprise, had been the responsibility of Adam Smith. 'The whole course of legislation, as well as the whole current of public opinion, had flowed in the same groove for centuries before the publication of *The Wealth of Nations*.'[3] In the heyday of England's political and economic power after 1850 it seemed that unfettered market forces, set free by enlightened governments inspired by wise economists, had 'caused' the industrial revolution. The expansion of England's international trade after the repeal of the Corn Laws confirmed this belief. After 1870, however, when England's leadership was increasingly challenged, the success of free enterprise was also questioned, and the debate about *laissez faire* became entangled in the political debate about the virtues and vices of modern capitalism.

1. *Lives of the Engineers: Vermuyden – Myddelton – Perry – James Brindley*, London, Murray, 1904 ed., p. xxiii.

2. *Lectures on the Industrial Revolution of the Eighteenth Century in England*, London, 1884, p. 85.

3. Adam Smith, *The Wealth of Nations*, edited by J. Thorold Rogers, London, 1869, p. xxv.

Adam Smith, also, was the inspiration and source of two other interpretations of the industrial revolution – that industrialization was the result of either increasing capital accumulation or increasing demand. In emphasizing the role of capital accumulation in English economic growth, some historians see as the cause of change the abundance of capital and the low rate of interest in eighteenth-century England. 'If we seek – it would be wrong to do so – for a single reason why the pace of economic development quickened about the middle of the eighteenth century', T. S. Ashton writes, 'it is to this we must look. The deep mines, solidly-built factories, well-constructed canals, and substantial houses of the industrial revolution were the products of relatively cheap capital.'[1] This view has received much encouragement from the literature, now vast, on economic development in which the economists in their theories of, and policies for, development have placed so much emphasis on capital formation. The emphasis on increasing demand as a prerequisite of growth can be traced back to another of Adam Smith's generalizations – that 'the division of labour is limited by the extent of the market' – but except for realizing that increasing international trade had helped England in the eighteenth century, the importance of increasing demand was largely explained away during the nineteenth century by the classical economists' belief that supply created its own demand.

Perhaps J. A. Hobson was the first modern writer to redress the balance, insisting in 1894 that industrialization was not possible without 'the existence of large, accessible markets with populations willing and economically able to consume the products of capitalist industry'.[2] Much later this argument was taken up by Miss E. W. Gilboy, who in a stimulating essay on 'Demand as a Factor in the Industrial Revolution'[3] asserted that increasing demand – from the expansion of foreign trade *and* from the rise of domestic population and incomes – was the key to eighteenth-century growth. 'Changing consumption

1. T. S. Ashton, *The Industrial Revolution, 1760–1850*, Oxford University Press, 1948, p. 11.

2. *The Evolution of Modern Capitalism*, London, 1894, p. 2.

3. *Facts and Factors in Economic History*, Harvard University Press, 1932, pp. 620–39.

standards, the increase of population and shifting of individuals from class to class, and a rise in real income provided a stimulus to the expansion of industry which must not be underestimated.'[1] Again, the modern economist has helped the historian: the Keynesian revolution has stressed the importance of consumer spending on profits and the incentive to invest. Growth has also been linked with increasing population and its potential effect on consumer demand. J. R. Hicks, for example, has suggested that 'perhaps the whole Industrial Revolution of the last two hundred years has been nothing else but a vast secular boom, largely induced by the unparalleled rise in population'.[2] But population by itself is obviously no necessary inducement to growth; the example of Ireland after 1750 is a painful demonstration that population can grow markedly with no development except in potato acreage. In England, however, the larger potential market – because of the growth of population, not only in Britain but also on the continent – was exploited by the entrepreneurs, and investment and development proceeded fast enough to outpace the rise in population and to increase the demand for labour faster than the supply.

The theories explaining English growth discussed so far have been economic. Other historians have eschewed economic explanations of historical change and, believing in the ideal foundations of all human endeavour, have seen in the making of the industrial revolution the working of non-economic factors: political theories, owing much to Locke, that emphasized 'the natural right of life, liberty and property' and thus provided the philosophic basis of *laissez faire*; a scientific revolution, beginning in the seventeenth century, that brought about 'a colossal secularization of thought in every possible realm of ideas',[3] as well as providing the necessary background of technical skill without which industrialization would have been impossible; new religions, stemming originally from the Reformation, that encouraged a spirit of rational self-interest, the driving ethos of capitalism;[4] a changing society whose *mores*

1. *Ibid.*, p. 639.

2. *Value and Capital*, Oxford University Press, 1939, p. 302.

3. H. Butterfield, *The Origins of Modern Science, 1300–1800*, London, 1949, Ch. 10.

4. See R. H. Tawney, *Religion and the Rise of Capitalism*, London, 1926.

and structure were flexible enough to allow entrepreneurial talent to break through its barriers and to innovate in economically significant enterprises. By the mid-eighteenth century these factors ensured that there was in England a progressive attitude towards change, a rational attitude towards work and wealth, and a healthy appetite for innovation. 'For two thousand years', H. Butterfield has written, 'the general appearance of the world and the activities of men had varied astonishingly little.... Now, however, change became so quick as to be perceptible to the naked eye, and the face of the earth and the activities of men were to alter more in a century than they had previously done in a thousand years.'[1]

In explaining the beginnings of the industrial revolution most historians have listed several causal factors, sometimes attempting an explanation in terms of a number of factors interacting over time, but more often settling for a simple one-cause model. But mono-causal explanations, however satisfying to the doctrinaire or tidy-minded, cannot explain such a complex event as the industrial revolution. What is necessary is a description of the economy before industrialization, in particular, an analysis of the factors that determined the rate of growth of output, followed by an evaluation of the strategic forces of change and how they operated to bring about industrialization and a rise in real incomes. The rate of growth of output was determined by the rate of growth of population, by changes in the technology and organization of agriculture and industry, and by the rate of capital accumulation. Some stimulus (or stimuli) – either internal and/or external – was sufficiently great to alter one or more of these major determinants, and thus to increase and sustain a higher rate of long-term economic growth. The most difficult problem is to determine the extent to which this stimulus was *exogenous* (i.e. independent of the economy) – for example, an increase in demand through international trade, or an autonomous growth of population or invention – and to what extent it was *endogenous* (i.e. generated within the economy) – for example, an increase in domestic capital accumulation, or the growth of population in response to economic incentives within the economy.

1. H. Butterfield, *op. cit.*, p. 187.

Both demographic theory and population history suggest that in the past the rate of growth of population tended to adapt itself to the demand for labour and/or the supply of food. In eighteenth-century England increased food supplies caused by a combination of good harvests after 1730 (quite fortuitous) and improving farming gave an initial impetus to population that was sustained by the mounting demand for labour of a more general economic expansion after the middle of the century. As regards capital accumulation it is probable also that the ability to save followed the incentive to invest; industry, for example, advanced less on loans than on the ploughing back of profits. Of course economic growth meant more capital equipment, but England was a rich country, with mature financial institutions, and there is little evidence that enterprise at any time in the eighteenth century was starved of capital. The important change in the eighteenth century was the use to which capital was put; less went into country houses and conspicuous consumption and more into factories, communications and trade; such a change represented a change in values rather than a significant change in the rate of capital accumulation. The history of invention links it less with economic motivation than with the growth of knowledge; innovation (the use of invention in economic enterprise), however, is largely economically determined. The coincidence in the 1780s of a sharp up-turn in industrial output and of a cluster of important technological innovations – the rotary-motion steam-engine, the puddling process for iron making, the perfection of cotton spinning machinery – proves that the increase in productivity was immediately the result of improved technology; and continued innovation after the 1780s, in technology and organization, sustained the rate of growth of productivity in English industry up to the fourth quarter of the nineteenth century. Dating the turning-point by technology fits in well with many economists' belief that growth is more intimately connected with technological change than with capital accumulation. England's wealth of entrepreneurial and industrial talent in this period, however, can be explained only in terms of an advanced society verging on greater development and stimulated into greater effort by widening opportunities and mutually reinforcing achievements. 'The new methods, new ideas and new departures of organization came to us not merely because we needed them', H. L. Beales writes, 'but because we wanted them and were well enough off to try them out and accept the changes they brought.'[1]

The sequence of events can now be described. The economy of England in the early eighteenth century, in comparison even with modern underdeveloped economies, was relatively advanced; in comparison with contemporary European economies, it had generally a higher level of real incomes; in agriculture there was persistent innovation (for example, in the use of fodder crops) and a sustained increase in agricultural output; in industry there was slow progress on a broad front, in textiles and tool making, in iron production and coal mining, and in construction, in response to slowly increasing domestic demand and a slowly increasing foreign trade; there was also a sophisticated commercial and financial structure, with the Bank of England, about twenty London banks and a dozen country banks by 1750. Population and food supplies were both increasing in 1700; by 1730, when the population of England and Wales was about 6 millions, the precarious balance between harvests and population was tipped permanently in favour of population by two decades of good harvests and low grain prices. 1730 marks one important turning point in the eighteenth century: partial depression in agriculture after 1730 was more than offset by continued progress in its efficient sectors (especially on the lighter soils) and by the increase in real incomes everywhere of food buyers who could afford to buy more industrial and colonial goods. What good harvests facilitated, general economic expansion after 1750 sustained. From the late forties there was a remarkable increase in foreign trade, particularly the export of manufactured goods to the colonies. At about the same time the rate of growth of population quickened, industrial production accelerated and there was widespread investment in agriculture and in communications, so that the decade 1750 to 1760 marked the first significant phase of the industrial revolution. In agriculture harvests were less bountiful and demand for foodstuffs greater than before 1750; in consequence prices were higher and the profit incentive to expand and improve production initiated enclosures and improved farming generally. In industry the market opportunities that induced expansion came from foreign

1. *The Industrial Revolution, 1750–1850. An Introductory Essay*, London, Cass, 1958 ed., p. 49.

trade and increasing domestic demand. After 1760 the rapid increase in country banks made for a national money market and the easier financing of trade, both internal and external. After 1760, also, the extension of the canal system made internal markets more accessible and had economy-wide effects on costs and incomes, further boosting demand. Thus after 1750 investment on a broad front – in agriculture, industry, trade and communications – set the stage for the great technical breakthroughs of the 1770s and 1780s which created profit opportunities in key industries of such magnitude that entrepreneurs responded quickly by rapidly increasing output. After 1780 the manufacturers of England reduced their costs of production so much that they were able to invade successfully the large markets of Europe. The expansion of output and trade in key sectors thereafter increased at a rate that well merited the adjective 'revolutionary'. The industrial revolution had begun.

III

W. W. Rostow has generalized from England's and other countries' experiences in industrialization that there is a clearly marked watershed in the growth process, a revolution 'tied directly to radical changes in methods of production, having their decisive consequences over a relatively short period of time'. This phenomenon Rostow has called, in a striking and now widely used phrase, 'the take-off into self-sustained growth'. 'The process of economic growth', he argues, 'can usefully be regarded as centering on a relatively brief interval of two or three decades when the economy and the society of which it is a part transform themselves in such ways that economic growth is, subsequently, more or less automatic.' At the centre of this process, as the 'powerful and essential engine of economic transformation', is 'the rapid growth of one or more new manufacturing sectors'.[1] Rostow sees, as the main condition of the take-off, a rise in the proportion of net investment to national income from under 5 per cent to a sustained over 10 per cent; this shift in the use of resources, concentrated in a few key new industries, he claims, explains both the initial increase

1. 'The Take-off into Self-sustained Growth', *Economic Journal*, Vol. LXVI, No. 261, March 1956, pp. 47, 25.

in productivity and the continuing increase. In the case of England Rostow's theses are incorrect: key industries led but growth was widespread with most industries benefiting; there was a clearly-marked turning point in growth about 1783, but no significant completion of growth in any aspect by 1802 (Rostow's dates); and the attainment of a net investment ratio of 10 per cent was not achieved for half a century, indeed until the massive investment in railways in the 1840s. The increase in productivity came more from an increase in the efficiency of capital goods than from an increase in the proportion of capital formation to national income. Capital formation was more the response of the growth of income than the creator of it; indeed, the limitations of the capital market made the self-financing of industry a necessity of growth.

The increased productivity of the economy was the result of a number of factors: (i) improved technology (for example, the substitution of steam for water power); (ii) the transfer of labour from less productive to more productive sectors of the economy, i.e. a change in the structure of the economy (for example, the transfer from agriculture to industry); (iii) the increased internal economies of scale of larger units of production, which allowed (*a*) the increased specialization of labour (for example, the hierarchy of specialized crafts in the textile mill), and (*b*) the improved organization of production (for example, the factory organization of industry with its reductions in transport costs and the overhead costs of buildings and machinery); (iv) the increased external economies of the localization of industry, with accessibility to increasing concentrations of labour and raw materials, and with the general increase in efficiency that came from improved communications and banking, and with the marketing economies of ports like Liverpool and Hull; (v) the taking-up of the slack of under- and un-employed resources in the economy and the use of a higher proportion of the working population in productive employment (for example, the more productive employment of women and children, which certainly increased production even if it also created social problems). The upward spiral of development was set in motion and sustained by the enlisting for development of existing resources and talents; once increased opportunities were created, the supply of capital and entrepreneurial talent proved elastic enough to be stimulated by the improved expectations, and growth was sustained by the creation and exploitation of further opportunities.

The economic consequences of industrialization are measurable. Today economic growth is usually measured by national income, but England's national income figures extend back reliably only a few decades. Nevertheless, some measure of aggregate growth can be inferred from contemporary estimates of national wealth that have been systematized recently by Phyllis Deane. These show that the national income (at current prices) of England and Wales in 1770 was *c.* £130m., and of Great Britain in 1800 was *c.* £230m., in 1830 *c.* £350m., and in 1850 *c.* £525m. Thus national income per head, at constant prices, increased over this period from something under £12 to about £24, i.e. average real income doubled. Over the nineteenth century, Phyllis Deane has calculated also that 'the real national income of Great Britain increased by a factor of about 14 . . . and that real national income per head roughly quadrupled'.[1] Given the statistical uncertainties of these figures, however, it is necessary to supplement them with data from sectors of the economy. Here the limitations are not as serious as might be supposed: the sectors that made up the bulk of the national product were fewer in 1800 than today and the data that has survived relates mainly to the sectors which were also the centres of technical change and rapid growth. There are, in addition, useful indices of total industrial output and of international trade. W. Hoffmann's index of industrial production shows that the annual percentage increase in the rate of growth of industrial output (including building) was much less than 2 per cent in the eighteenth century before 1780, but was between 3 and 4 per cent from 1780 to 1792 and from 1818 to 1855, and from 2 to 3 per cent during the Revolutionary and Napoleonic Wars and from 1856 to 1876.[2] Foreign trade grew even more spectacularly: W. Schlote reckoned that the annual average percentage increase in the rate of growth of overseas trade was 1·2 per cent from 1700 to 1770, 4·9 per cent from 1780 to 1800, and after a decline during the war, 4·4 per

1. *British Economic Growth, 1688–1959*, pp. 279, 282.

2. *British Industry, 1700–1950*, translated by W. O. Henderson and W. H Chaloner, Oxford (Blackwell), 1955.

cent from 1821 to 1851.[1] By 1830 industrial production contributed one-third of the British national income and foreign trade equalled in value about one-tenth of national income; both were vitally important to the national economy and its growth.

The statistics of particular industries confirm these general trends. For the late eighteenth century, T. S. Ashton writes: 'After 1782 almost every statistical series of production shows a sharp upward turn. More than half the growth in the shipments of coal and the mining of copper, more than three-quarters of the increase of broadcloths, four-fifths of that of printed cloth, and nine-tenths of the exports of cotton goods were concentrated in the last eighteen years of the century.'[2] The output of candles, soap, textiles, coal and iron all moved upwards in the eighties; of 2,600 patents for the century, more than half were registered after 1780; the eighties was the decade of the first dramatic increase in the number of country banks; it was prefaced by the completion in 1777 of the Grand Trunk Canal which linked the Midlands with the Mersey. In the iron industry expansion was made possible by Henry Cort's process for the manufacture of iron, using coke instead of charcoal, and by James Watt's rotary-motion steam-engine which made available the blast necessary for coke smelting. Applied widely first in South Wales, the puddling process had spread to Yorkshire by 1790 and to Northumberland and Durham by the end of the century. In 1797 England became, for the first time, an exporter of iron; by 1812 exports exceeded imports; from 1800 to 1850 about 20 per cent of the pig-iron produced in England was exported. The number of blast furnaces increased from under 20 in 1760, to over 80 by 1790; in 1805 there were 177, in 1830, 372 and in 1852, 655; after 1800 the majority were coke-fired. The production of pig-iron was about 30,000 tons in 1770, 250,000 tons by 1805, 650,000 tons by 1830 and 2 million tons by 1850. In the cotton industry, growth was even more spectacular. James Hargreaves (the jenny), Richard Arkwright (the water frame) and Samuel Crompton (the mule) between them had perfected the machine spinning of cotton by 1780. The average import of

1. *British Overseas Trade from 1700 to the 1930s*, translated by W. O. Henderson and W. H. Chaloner, Oxford (Blackwell), 1952.

2. *An Economic History of England, The Eighteenth Century*, London, 1955, p. 125.

raw cotton from 1776 to 1780 was 7·65 m. lbs.; from 1786 to 1790, 25·5 m. lbs.; from 1796 to 1800, 37·5 m. lbs.; from 1801 to 1805, 58·5 m. lbs. In 1815 the import of cotton was *c.* 100 m. lbs., in 1830 *c.* 250 m. lbs, and in 1850 *c.* 620 m. lbs. The number of cotton spindles totalled less than 2 millions in 1780, more than 4m. in 1800, 10m. in 1830 and 21m. in 1850; power looms were introduced into the industry rapidly after 1820, with 50,000 looms in 1830 and 250,000 in 1850. By 1830 the cotton industry employed 500,000 people, of whom about half were already in factories, and exported 445 m. yards of cloth and 65 m. lbs. of yarn, about 50 per cent of the total production of the industry and constituting about 40 per cent of the total value of all British exports.

The factory growth of both the iron and cotton industries depended on coal and communications. England was already unique in Europe at the beginning of the eighteenth century for the amount of coal consumed, and over the century output rose gradually from 3 to 10 million tons. Coal was the first raw material in history to be measured in millions of tons; the steam-engine was evolved largely to solve the technical problems of haulage and drainage in coal-mines; the eighteenth-century canals were built primarily to transport coal; coal was the fuel that enabled the rapid expansion of the iron industry (and iron was the basic structural and engineering material of industrialization) and the manufacture of bricks (the building material that enabled housing to keep pace with the growth of population). 'The decisive technological change which freed so many industries from dependence upon organic raw materials', E. A. Wrigley writes, 'was the discovery of a way of using coal where once wood had been essential.'[1] Iron, produced by coke, replaced wood in shafts, gears, wheels and machines, and was used increasingly in civil engineering (e.g. bridges); the new industrial towns were built of bricks. Coal production increased from *c.* 10 m. tons in 1800 to *c.* 25 m. tons by 1830, to *c.* 50 m. tons by 1850. Coal was used both for domestic and industrial purposes; one of the most important industrial users was the steam-engine. Before Watt, in 1781, patented a rotary motion which gave the steam-engine universality for the production and use of indus-

1. 'The Supply of Raw Materials in the Industrial Revolution'. *Economic History Review*, 2nd ser., Vol. XV, No. 2, 1962, p. 4.

trial power, it had been used almost exclusively for the lifting of water – in mines and brine works, for industrial water wheels and for the supply of water to London. By 1800 there were probably 1,000 steam engines at work in England; of these about 250 were in the cotton industry, showing that steam power had already spread widely into other industries. Thereafter, and especially after the lapsing of Watt's patent in 1800, steam power increasingly replaced human, animal, wind and water power wherever it was economically appropriate. By 1838, for example, the cotton industry was using 46,000 steam horse-power and the woollen industry 17,000; by 1850 the combined textile use was almost 100,000 horse-power.

In 1830, it has been calculated, Britain was producing three-quarters of Europe's mined coal, half of Europe's cotton goods and iron, and most of Europe's steam-engines. Without improved communications, there would have been a limit to the size of markets for these growing industries, a generally higher cost structure, and wider disparity between the development of different parts of the country. Before the great rise in population after 1780 canals probably increased market potentialities more than the increase in population. Adam Smith wrote, for example: 'Good roads, canals and navigable rivers, by diminishing the expense of carriage, put the remote parts of the country nearly on a level with those in the neighbourhood of the town; they are, upon that account, the greatest of all improvements.' An extensive network of communications, indeed, is one of the greatest economic blessings which any country can have. Before the building of canals, long haulage of bulk goods was achieved by coastal traffic and river navigation, and there were already in 1750 about 1,000 miles of navigable waterways in England. The first canals were completed in Lancashire – in 1757 at St. Helen's and in 1761 at Manchester, both to haul coal – and by 1850 there were over 4,000 miles of canals in England, linking the main industrial towns, coal-fields, rivers and ports. Nearly 3,000 miles were constructed *before* 1800, thus providing in the initial stage of the industrial revolution the unification of the English market that was essential for growth. The importance of railways was even greater, but few were constructed before 1835, and the first large extension of lines occurred between 1840 and 1850 when 5,000 miles of railway were put into operation. The importance of

railways was greater after 1850 than before, but the massive investment and large employment that were required to build and maintain railways had already altered the economic structure of England by 1850. Railways greatly reduced the time of travel (probably 75 per cent), lowered transport costs, extended communications beyond the canal network, increased labour mobility and further concentrated population and enterprise. Railways also encouraged the habit of investment and by 1850, for the first time in history, an economy was devoting a net tenth or more of its total income to capital accumulation. The embodiment of new technology in capital goods on this scale explains how Britain became 'the workshop of the world'.

It is difficult to say how positive a role the growth of banking played in the industrial revolution. Certainly money and credit were needed in increasing quantities, and they were provided by the rapid growth of banks in London and in the country. Banks, however, provided little of the long-term capital that was needed by agriculture, transport and industry. Banking developed initially for the deposit and loan of money, but after 1760 the proliferation of banks was stimulated by a growing demand for short-term credit for working capital for industry, for the inter-regional and international transfer of funds to settle trading debts, and for cash (in the form of bank-notes). There were 100 country banks by 1780, 370 in 1800, 554 in 1826 and 311 in 1842, after which time their numbers declined rapidly as they were absorbed into joint-stock banks with branches. Together with the London banks they formed, even in 1780, a network of credit that extended from the agricultural districts where there were surpluses through London to the new industrial areas of the Midlands and North. The country banks have been much criticized for their speculative excesses – 'a perpetual menace to economic tranquillity' – but a liberal credit policy was more conducive to growth than a restrictive policy would have been, and so the banks provided essential and stimulating service to industry and trade at a critical stage of development.

The industrial revolution changed both the way of earning a living and the way of life of the English. Briefly, in terms of employment, the results were as follows: the proportion of the labour force engaged in agriculture declined from 40 to 45 per

cent in 1780, to 35 per cent in 1801, to 24 per cent in 1831, to 21 per cent in 1851; over the same period the proportion in manufacturing, mining and building increased from 25 to 42 per cent; trade and transport, which accounted for 10 per cent of employment in 1801, did not significantly change its proportion until the railways were built. Proportions, however, in a population that rose from 9 millions in 1800 to 18 millions in 1850, disguise absolute growth. To feed the large increase in non-agricultural labour it was necessary, before the rapid rise in food imports that began in the 1840s, to increase domestic food production. This was achieved both by maintaining agriculture still in 1850 as the largest single English industry whose total employment had increased continuously to that date, and by increasing agricultural productivity. Not only were there more agricultural workers, but the acreage of arable had increased (especially during the wars) and productivity had increased markedly. For example, a rising wheat yield (from *c.* 20 to *c.* 30 bushels per acre between 1800 and 1850) and a large increase in the output of livestock were the result of greatly increased long-term investment in agriculture. There was greater attention to cultivation, better drainage, a considerable improvement in the range and acreage of fodder crops planted in rotation, the heavier stocking and richer manuring of arable, and the extension of stock-fattening on arable farms. During the wars, indeed, when so much labour was diverted to the army, the blockade ensured that agriculture, temporarily, proportionately increased its contribution to national income; it ensured also an agricultural expansion that made the feeding of England possible in the next period of rapid growth of industrial population in towns. Manufacturing industry increased its work force most in the decades after Waterloo, so that by 1831 about one-third of England's working population was in industry, a proportion that remained stable during the rest of the nineteenth century. As significant as the changing proportions of employment was the growth of towns. For centuries towns had been spread fairly evenly over the English countryside, their siting and size (with the exception of London) determined largely by agriculture. Now population became concentrated in larger towns and cities in the Midlands and North. In 1800 London already had nearly 900,000 inhabitants, but all other towns in England and Wales were tiny by comparison, there being only 14 with populations of over 20,000. By 1851 London had grown to 2,362,236, there were 54 cities with populations of between 20,000 and 100,000, and seven with over 100,000 (Birmingham, Bradford, Bristol, Leeds, Liverpool, Manchester, Sheffield). The pattern of population distribution clearly reflected the changes in industry, with population concentrated increasingly either on coal-fields or at great ports, or in the metropolis.

The concentration of population was the result of migration from rural to urban areas, not of significant differences in natural increase or mortality between areas: of the general increase in population an increasing proportion was attracted to the growing towns. This might suggest that the population increase was closely connected with the process of industrialization, but since the population increase was European-wide in an economic environment which, except for England, was still in 1830 predominantly agricultural, it is impossible to argue that in England alone the increase in numbers was specifically the result of industrialization. However, since the rate of growth of population in England was the greatest in Europe, it is certain that the industrial revolution influenced the pace at which population grew. A plausible sequence is the quickening of European population in the eighteenth century, mainly because of a general increase in the supply of foodstuffs, the result of agricultural improvements over a wide area, followed in England by an industrial revolution which increased both the supply of consumer goods and the opportunities for employment. More people survived; more were able to find work. The combination in England of improving agriculture and industrialization was in this period unique; so too was the rate of increase of the English population. But was this increase the consequence of decreased mortality, increased birth-rate, or both? The evidence indicates both that a falling death-rate was the main determinant of change, and also that the fall could not have been the result of medical improvements which did not add significantly to the power to survive until the third quarter of the nineteenth century. Economic advance initiated and sustained the increase in numbers, providing the food and other consumer goods, and the employment, which were necessary to support a larger population. There were, in particular, improvements in diet, in hygiene and in clothing. One important food that supplemented diets, in northern England as well as in Ireland and on the continent, was the potato; indeed, Roscher, the great German economist, declared unequivocally that the increasing consumption of the potato was *the* cause of the increased rate of growth of European population. Economic development was rapid enough to outpace the rise in population. Thus J. S. Mill could write of the period after 1820 that population had not pressed on subsistence, and that, instead, 'subsistence and employment in England [had] never increased more rapidly'.[1]

IV

What were the long-term results of the industrial revolution? M. Dobb has written that 'in the nineteenth century, the *tempo* of economic change, as regards the structure of industry and of social relationships, the volume of output and the extent and variety of trade, was entirely abnormal, judged by the standards of previous centuries'.[2] The result of the industrial revolution was a vast enlargement and cheapening of production, in agriculture, industry and services, as well as in trade and consumption. This increase in production was achieved by a revolution in technology and organization, by the use of complicated machinery, by the exploitation of new sources of power and by the increasing concentration of production in larger and better administered units. There was also a remarkable growth of science and the spread and deepening of education. In terms of organization, the factory became increasingly the dominant physical form of industrial enterprise and the joint stock company the dominant financial form. The two were linked – because of the need to finance large-scale production, with its aggregation of buildings, equipment and people, and large-scale trade, with its complications of international and interregional payments – by the development of banking, and of capital, discount and money markets. Labour was massed into industrial cities (as less people produced more food in agriculture, and as food and raw material imports increased), and urban society, with its factories and slums, with its self-conscious and organized proletariat, became the focus of political as well

1. *The Principles of Political Economy*, 5th ed., 1862, p. 161.

2. *Studies in the Development of Capitalism*, London, 1946, p. 256.

as of economic life. Specialization led to an increasing dependence on trade, made possible by the growth of communications, and to a pattern of highly complex exchanges between individuals, between regions and between nations. The total result was, in the long run, undoubtedly beneficial, with the mass of English workers in 1900 enjoying a substantially higher standard of living than their forefathers had enjoyed before industrialization.

On the short-term results of the industrial revolution, however, interpretation has been dominated by a social costs rather than by an economic gains theory. Certainly English society was much changed, even by 1830, as a result of industrialization. Toynbee stressed, for example, 'a great social revolution, a change in the balance of political power and in the relative position of classes', and argued that personal relationships in industry had been destroyed, and that the 'cash nexus' had been substituted for the 'human tie', opening wide the floodgates of exploitation. 'We all know the horrors that ensued in England before it was restrained by legislation and combination,' he concluded.[1] Influential writers like the Hammonds reinforced Toynbee's conclusions with detailed studies of village, town and skilled labourers. These writers, preoccupied with contemporary social problems, certain that urban life compared unfavourably with rural life, indignant about the lack of protection of labour in the harsh *laissez faire* society of industrial England, were convinced that conditions of life had deteriorated under industrialization. In the last thirty years, however, in spite of the continued popularity of the critics of the industrial revolution, powerful attacks against the pessimistic view by two great economic historians, J. H. Clapham and T. S. Ashton, have converted most historians to the view that the industrial revolution in England benefited the workers, not only in the long run, but also in the short run. Since between 1780 and 1850 average *per capita* real income increased, since there was no trend in the distribution of income against the workers, since after 1815 prices fell while wages remained constant, since *per capita* consumption of food and other consumer goods increased, and since government intervened increasingly in economic and social life to protect and improve

1. A. Toynbee, *Lectures on the Industrial Revolution of the Eighteenth Century in England*, London, 1884, pp. 72–73.

living and working conditions, then the real wages of the majority of English workers were rising throughout the industrial revolution. This is not to say that the standard of living was *high*, even in 1900, nor that it was rising *fast* at any time before 1850, nor that there was no dire poverty, or no serious cyclical and technological unemployment. But to admit the existence of distress is not to deny the upward trend in living standards, nor the opportunities created by industrialization.

Considering the magnitude of the economic changes, it is not surprising that they were accompanied by equally profound social and political change. Indeed, perhaps in no other period of English history was change so rapid, and at no other time did the rapidly changing pattern of social, economic and political life raise so many acutely disturbing problems. Never since the Commonwealth did England experience such intensity and diversity of thought; at no other period in English history were so many poor men raised to wealth and distinction. England buzzed with new men and new ideas. The working class, liberated for the first time in their history from the servility and patronage of rural society, found themselves free to organize and argue, to bring their massive support to their own defence. 'Systematic and widespread discontent' there certainly was; it arose from the clearer recognition of social ills, from the ability of the working class to organize themselves into protective organizations, and from reasoned discontent about the distribution of wealth. And, it is important to remember, working-class aspirations were encouraged by those middle-class reformers who combined humanitarianism, utilitarianism and a 'ferocious goodness'. The result was, as Macaulay claimed in 1830, 'the most enlightened generation of the most enlightened people that ever existed'. Thus the industrial revolution in England not only brought greater wealth to the worker, it also stimulated social and political reform, and encouraged that optimism and belief in progress that became characteristic of the nineteenth century.

SELECT BIBLIOGRAPHY

There are two classics which should be consulted by all students of the Industrial Revolution:

A. Toynbee, *Lectures on the Industrial Revolution of the Eighteenth Century in England* (London, 1884); and

P. Mantoux, *The Industrial Revolution in the Eighteenth Century* (London, English translation, 1928);

and one which should be compulsory reading:

T. S. Ashton, *The Industrial Revolution* (Oxford, 1948).

On the background to the Industrial Revolution see:

C. Wilson, *England's Apprenticeship, 1603–1763* (London, 1965).

M. W. Flinn, *The Origins of the Industrial Revolution* (London, 1966).

R. M. Hartwell, *The Causes of the Industrial Revolution* (London, 1967).

The most recent important work will be found in the journal:

The Economic History Review (published by the Economic History Society).

Older general works of interest are:

A. P. Usher, *The Industrial History of England* (Cambridge, Mass., 1920);

W. Bowden, *Industrial Society in England towards the End of the Eighteenth Century* (New York, 1925; 2nd edition, Cass, London, 1965);

J. L. and B. Hammond, *The Rise of Modern Industry* (London, 1925);

C. R. Fay, *Great Britain from Adam Smith to the Present Day* (Cambridge, 1928);

H. L. Beales, *The Industrial Revolution, 1750–1850* (London, 1958 edition).

Contributions by economists include:

E. A. G. Robinson, 'The Changing Structure of the British Economy', *Economic Journal*, LXIV (1954);

Phyllis Deane and W. A. Cole, *British Economic Growth, 1688–1959. Trends and Structure* (Cambridge, 1962).

R. M. Hartwell, *The Industrial Revolution and Economic Growth* (1971).

Good general text-books are:

W. H. B. Court, *A Concise Economic History of Britain from 1760 to Recent Times* (Cambridge, 1954); and

A. Redford, *The Economic History of England 1760–1860* (London, 2nd edition, 1960).

P. Deane, *The First Industrial Revolution* (Cambridge, 1965);

P. Mathias, *The First Industrial Nation* (London, 1969).

For industrial studies see:

H. D. Fong, *Triumph of Factory System in England* (Tientsin, 1930);

W. Hoffmann, *British Industry, 1700–1950* (Oxford, English translation, 1955);

S. Pollard, *The Genesis of Modern Management. A Study of the Industrial Revolution in England* (1965).

A. E. Musson, *Science Technology and Economic Growth in the Eighteenth Century* (London, 1972).

and the detailed bibliographies of

B. R. Mitchell and P. Deane, *Abstract of British Historical Statistics* (Cambridge, 1962).

For agriculture see:

B. H. Slicher van Bath, *The Agrarian History of Western Europe, A.D. 500–1850* (London, English translation, 1963).

J. D. Chambers & G. E. Mingay, *The Agricultural Revolution, 1750–1850* (1966);

E. L. Jones, *Agriculture and Economic Growth in England, 1650–1815* (1967).

On trade see:

W. Schlote, *British Overseas Trade from 1700 to the 1930's* (Oxford, English translation, 1952); and

A. H. Imlah, *Economic Elements in the Pax Britannica* (Cambridge, Mass., 1958).

On banking see:

J. H. Clapham, *The Bank of England: a History* (Cambridge, 2 vols., 1944); and

L. S. Pressnell, *Country Banking in the Industrial Revolution* (Oxford, 1956).

On population see:

H. J. Habakkuk, 'The Economic History of Modern Britain,' *Journal of Economic History*, XVIII (1958);

J. T. Krause, 'Some Neglected Factors in the English Industrial Revolution', *Journal of Economic History*, XIX (1959); and

T. McKeown and R. G. Brown, 'Medical Evidence related to English Population Changes in the Eighteenth Century', *Population Studies*, IX (1955).

D. V. Glass & D. E. C. Eversley (eds.), *Population in History. Essays in Historical Demography* (1965).

On technology see:

A. P. Usher, *A History of Mechanical Inventions* (Cambridge, Mass., revised edition, 1954); and

Charles Singer and others, *A History of Technology*, vol. IV, *The Industrial Revolution. c. 1750 to c. 1850* (Oxford, 1958).

On labour conditions see the 'labourer' volumes of J. L. and B. Hammond; also

E. J. Hobsbawm, *Labouring Men. Studies in the History of Labour* (London, 1964),

E. P. Thompson, *The Making of the English Working Class* (London, 1963), and

criticisms of the pessimistic interpretation by T. S. Ashton, *op. cit.*, and

R. M. Hartwell, *The Industrial Revolution and Economic Growth* (London, 1971).

For interesting regional studies see:

W. H. B. Court, *The Rise of the Midland Industries, 1600–1830* (Oxford, 1938);

A. H. John, *The Industrial Development of South Wales, 1750–1850* (Cardiff, 1950); and

J. D. Chambers, *The Vale of Trent, 1670–1800* (Economic History Review Supplement, 1957).

For statistics of the period see Mitchell and Deane, *op. cit.*; and for contemporary sources see J. B. Williams, *A Guide to the Printed Materials for English Social and Economic History, 1750–1850* (New York, 2 vols., 1926).